Christopher Isherwood

by

CAROLYN G. HEILBRUN

Columbia University Press
NEW YORK & LONDON 1970

COLUMBIA ESSAYS ON MODERN WRITERS

is a series of critical studies of English, Continental, and other writers whose works are of contemporary artistic and intellectual significance.

Editor

William York Tindall

Advisory Editors

Jacques Barzun   W. T. H. Jackson   Joseph A. Mazzeo

Christopher Isherwood is Number 53 of the series

CAROLYN G. HEILBRUN
is Associate Professor of English at Columbia University.

Acknowledgment is made to the following for permission to quote from works by Christopher Isherwood: to Random House, for permission to quote extracts from *Prater Violet* (copyright 1945 by Christopher Isherwood), *The Condor and the Cows* (copyright 1948, 1949 by Christopher Isherwood), and *Journey to a War;* to Simon & Schuster, Inc., for permission to quote extracts from *A Single Man* (copyright © 1964 by Christopher Isherwood) and *Down There on a Visit* (copyright © 1959, 1961 by Christopher Isherwood); and to Curtis Brown, Ltd., for permission to quote extracts from *The Memorial, Lions and Shadows,* and *The Berlin Stories* (copyright © 1945, 1954 by New Directions).

Christopher Isherwood

Since Christopher Isherwood has been denied, or spared, the gifts of widespread fame or fashion, it is appropriate to begin with the pronouncement that he is the best British novelist of his generation. "Generation," to be sure, must be conceived in its narrowest sense: those born in the twentieth century before World War I. Neither as witty as Waugh's nor as intense as Orwell's, his fictions have achieved the integrity of art while illuminating the human tensions of our time. Muted in tone, self-effacing in manner, his works continue to make a quiet but persistent claim on our attention. One wishes him to be better known, not for his sake, but for ours.

"Once you care about what he writes," Angus Wilson has written, "you care strongly enough to read everything that he produces." To read, for example, his "autobiographical" *Lions and Shadows*, is to find oneself not only committed to the reading of all his other books but surprised into an appreciation of the rarest literary conjunction of our times: readability and high intelligence. Cyril Connolly has referred to Isherwood's "fatal readability": nothing which can be read with such ease and pleasure will be accorded high marks. Readability is usually allied with superficiality, best-sellerdom, or, at best, competent nonfiction, and there can be little doubt that Isherwood's readability has preserved him from academic sanctification. It is difficult to be properly serious about a writer in whose literary presence one feels so relaxed.

Frank Kermode's is a typical attitude: "I remember," he has written, "the excitement when *Sally Bowles* came out, and my despondency when it lasted no longer than the lecture during which I read it. It is still read in the same way, for fun. And Mr. Norris is, so far as I know, the only character of thirties fiction with any of the old Dickensian extra-fictional prestige." But, Mr. Kermode adds: "Mr. Isherwood is not serious." Isherwood's friend W. H. Auden has spoken of the necessity for the artist to combine frivolity and earnestness, since "without frivolity he becomes a bore, without earnestness an aesthete." *With* frivolity, however, as both Auden and Isherwood must have learned, a writer runs the danger of being considered not serious at all.

Certainly the effect of ease in Isherwood's writing is deluding: it persuades the reader to overlook the enormous skill of his prose. Carefully wrought prose is of two sorts: Joycean, artistically contrived to force the reader into attention and linguistic discovery; and documentary, allowing the reader ease, even inattention, until he is struck by the emotional and moral implications of what he has passively absorbed.

The word "documentary" is unsatisfactory but probably irreplaceable. As G. S. Fraser has said, "Isherwood must stand alone for what is either a lost species, or one that only evolved into fully satisfying life in his own works." No one, in these works, is romanticized, condemned, or even judged; if the narrator, named Christopher Isherwood, responds at all, he does so only from personal pique or inconvenience. The brilliantly unobtrusive prose allows us to watch violence, brutality, and compromise with pain, and to realize only when the book is finished that in doing so we, like the narrator, have failed in humanity. Isherwood's Berlin Stories are the best rendering of early Hitler Germany we have: an artistic re-creation of a society's self-betrayal.

Today the sun is brilliantly shining; it is quite mild and warm.

[4]

I go out for my last morning walk, without an overcoat or hat. The sun shines, and Hitler is master of this city. The sun shines, and dozens of my friends—my pupils at the Workers' School, the men and women I met at the I.A.H.—are in prison, possibly dead. But it isn't of them that I am thinking—the clear-headed ones, the purposeful, the heroic; they recognized and accepted the risks. I am thinking of poor Rudi, in his absurd Russian blouse. Rudi's make-believe, story-book game has become earnest; the Nazis won't laugh at him; they'll take him on trust for what he pretended to be. Perhaps at this very moment Rudi is being tortured to death.

I catch sight of my face in the mirror of a shop, and am horrified to see that I am smiling. You can't help smiling, in such beautiful weather. The trams are going up and down the Kleiststrasse, just as usual. They, and the people on the pavement, and the teacosy dome of the Nollendorfplatz station have an air of curious familiarity, of striking resemblance to something one remembers as normal and pleasant in the past—like a very good photograph.

No. Even now I can't altogether believe that any of this has really happened.

Sally Bowles and Mr. Norris made Isherwood's name in the literary world of the thirties. *The Last of Mr. Norris* (published in England as *Mr. Norris Changes Trains*) and *Sally Bowles*, appearing in 1935 and 1937, introduced not only Isherwood's brilliant though cool evocation of Hitler Germany, but also that "ventriloquist's dummy" "Christopher Isherwood," whose phrase "I am a camera" the playwright John Van Druten was to make properly famous decades later. It was not unnatural that many people took the character "Christopher Isherwood" (called William Bradshaw, Isherwood's middle names, in *The Last of Mr. Norris*) to be a portrait of the author; the confusion between the author and his persona deepened with the publication of *Lions and Shadows*, which, although presented as an autobiography, was in truth another documentary of an English upper-class "education in the twenties."

[5]

James Joyce once remarked how difficult everything is "when your life and your work make one." This is a difficulty which Isherwood, contrary to appearances, has avoided. Although he has stated that his work is "all part of an autobiography," his is the autobiography, not of a personality or individual, but of the events that individual encountered in his lifetime. What "happened" to the character "Christopher Isherwood" happened, in more or less the same way, to the author, but the inner man to whom things happened is not the character. Isherwood, therefore, has written, in the continuing "autobiography" of his namesake, a biography of his time. Continuing through many documentaries, the biography has by now, Isherwood tells us, been completed, *Down There on a Visit* (1962) being the last appearance of the dummy. By following the events in the life of this dummy, we can trace most of the major external occurrences in the author's life and, more importantly, some of the major historical forces of our century.

Here, then, is the life the two Christopher Isherwoods share: They were born in 1904. Their father was killed in World War I while they were at preparatory school being imbued with notions about the virtues and glories of the men at the front. They met W. H. Auden at this school. After public school (Repton) where they came to know "Allen Chalmers," the Isherwoods went up to Cambridge where, together with Chalmers, they began to conceive of the established world as the enemy, and to invent and write about a grotesque world in which they virtually had their being. (Chalmers, whose real name is Edward Upward, has published the only extant example of these writings, a story entitled "The Railway Accident," complete with introduction by Isherwood.) Determined to be sent down from Cambridge for an unforgivable crime, the

Isherwoods answered the questions on the tripos in limericks. Day in and day out, the Isherwoods had brooded on what they called "the Test"; they had missed the war, could they in fact meet any brutal physical challenge? The tests of the established society they passed all too easily, but what of war and violence? They bought a motorcycle and made themselves ride it with the throttle open for the count of a hundred.

Sent down from Cambridge, they worked for a time as secretary to a string quartet, and as a private tutor ("If you are under thirty, and have an educated voice, a shaven chin and a clean neck, you should have no difficulty getting a tutoring job at any time"). In 1928 they decided to become a medical student; it was, after all, something to do. Their first novel, *All the Conspirators*, about a family war between the generations, had just been published but would not achieve sufficient notice or sales to encourage novel-writing as a way to earn a living. Medical school lasted for two semesters, and then Auden, who was living in Berlin, encouraged the Isherwoods to join him. They decided to settle in Berlin, to support themselves by giving English lessons, to write another novel, *The Memorial*, and to observe life in that most decadent of cities.

Hitler's coming to power made them a refugee; they traveled. For a time, returning to London, they worked on a film with Berthold Viertel. Their final prewar visit to England coincided with the Munich crisis, and in the stress of this, acting upon a previous decision to settle in the United States, they came to Hollywood, worked for the movies, and became a Vedantist. They had, with Auden, visited China in 1938, and they traveled through South America in 1948. They have since revisited England and Berlin, live in California, and are not married.

Isherwood's personal, private, emotional autobiography has

not, except for one essay, been published. And even there, in his account of "An Approach to Vedanta" where he was prepared to tell a personal story in the hope that such revelations might be of use to others in their search for certitude, he has omitted any personal details which could possibly be considered extraneous. In describing, for example, his "exaggerated reactions" to the Christianity he was exposed to in his boyhood, he mentions "certain experiences . . . which had given me a dread of authority. Certainly, my violence on the subject approached hysteria. But this isn't important, as far as my present narrative is concerned." The family pressures of his boyhood have never been revealed, nor has the size of his family. Those of his readers whom Isherwood anticipates in *Exhumations* as interested "in my writings and, hence, in me" discover little about "me." In two rather extended personal interviews, Isherwood has revealed remarkably little about himself.

There is, of course, no reason why he should do so. But it is essential to emphasize, in any discussion of an author who appears to put himself into everything he writes, often by name, that in fact the life and the work are *not* one, as Joyce's were. There remains one personal thing to be said, not so much about Isherwood's life as about his personality. It is extraordinary, in these days unique, to find a man who has never published a single word that is nasty, carping, mean, or destructive. He might, perhaps, be accused of being insufficiently critical in the writing of reviews. Doubtless he would agree with Auden who has said that one cannot write a bad review without showing off, and that the only reason for reviewing books is to draw attention to some work which might otherwise not be sufficiently appreciated. Although Isherwood frequently reveals the pettiest of motives in the dummy Chris,

[8]

the man is never petty—never, that is, in his published self. Nor is this a new characteristic, post-Vedantist, for example. His religious conversion appears to be, in the light of all his work, what F. H. Bradley has called the finding of reasons for what we believe upon instinct. Isherwood's quality of gentleness—encompassing the entire etymology of that word—might not deserve so studied a notice were it not so rare a quality.

This personal goodness is, in fact, a noticeable quality in only one other English author, E. M. Forster, whose influence upon Isherwood has been marked. Forster was a member of the earlier, Bloomsbury generation which saw art and personal relations as opposed to politics. As Stephen Spender has said, "Forster had no enthusiasm for the liberated, materially better world which he felt bound to support." Isherwood, essentially Forsterian, nonetheless belonged to the generation which passed, in his own words, "into a socially-conscious political phase" at the beginning of the thirties. "We wanted to point the way to a happier era of peace and plenty, equality and civil justice." It was only in 1939, therefore, that Isherwood, crossing to America on a boat with Auden, realized, at sea, that he, like Forster, had always essentially been a pacifist. Typically, Forster, who had never wanted a war, was the only one in England at the time of the Munich crisis who was not terrified or hysterical with excitement. In *Down There on a Visit* Forster is described at the time when the newspapers were comparing Chamberlain to Abe Lincoln and Jesus Christ:

My England is E.M.; the antiheroic hero, with his straggly straw mustache, his light, gay, blue baby eyes and his elderly stoop. Instead of a folded umbrella or a brown uniform, his emblems are his tweed cap (which is too small for him) and the odd-shaped brown paper parcels in which he carries his belongings from country to town and back again. While the others tell their followers to be ready to die, he advises us to live as though we were

[9]

immortal. And he really does this himself, although he is as anxious and afraid as any of us, and never for an instant pretends not to be. He and his books and what they stand for are all that is truly worth saving from Hitler; and the vast majority of people on this island aren't even aware that he exists.

Isherwood and Auden, in coming to America as England stood on the brink of war, laid themselves open to enormous abuse from those left behind. In fact, both men had earlier planned to emigrate from England; both offered their services when war came. Isherwood, moreover, had scarcely lived in England for any length of time since his early twenties. Yet, as John Lehmann has written, "Christopher and Wystan were suddenly branded as traitors and cowards in a campaign that was waged with the utmost fury against them in dailies and weeklies, respectable as well as less respectable; questions were asked in Parliament, scathing judgements were passed on them under privilege by people who may never have more than glanced at their works." Only Forster, Lehmann tells us, was always anxious "to hear the latest news I had from Christopher, to whom he remained unswervingly loyal through all the public outbreaks of hostility."

It is, incidentally, characteristic of the influence of Forster, to whom they dedicated *Journey to a War* in a now famous sonnet by Auden, that Isherwood and Auden, having settled on opposite shores of the United States, having each adopted a religion incomprehensible to the other, could remain friends. When Auden was asked how he and Isherwood collaborated, the answer was, "With the greatest politeness." And he was later to add that while one could have a friend who believed in Vedanta, one could not have a friend who liked his steak well-done. In short, they had both, deserting their generation, left reform behind them.

Forster's literary influence upon Isherwood is easily noticeable. From Isherwood's first decision to learn from Forster to "tea-table" or underplay it, the influence of Forster's novels and essays can be discerned. Isherwood also shares what Lionel Trilling has called Forster's refusal to be great. But too much must not be made of this. It is impossible to imagine Forster creating Sally Bowles. And for Isherwood, Forster's "Love, the Beloved Republic" was impossible without a religious faith to sustain it.

Unique in creating and perfecting the documentary form, Isherwood, perhaps because of the distance from his subject that form provided, was also the only writer of his time to explore the English phenomenon of male homosexuality. Not, indeed, until Michael Holroyd's biography of Lytton Strachey was the subject so central to English intellectual life treated in a manner neither maudlin nor flamboyant. Isherwood has understood and presented the various forms of homosexuality no less calmly and keenly than he has re-created the rise of the Nazis or the hideous fascination with war of his generation in England.

Diana Trilling, in a discussion of stunning insight, has shown how a man like J. R. Ackerley, in *My Father and Myself*, revealed the extent to which England escaped the many sexual guilts named by Freud and so eagerly absorbed by America into her culture. Mrs. Trilling points out that Ackerley emerges as more "manly" than Phillip Roth's Portnoy, with whom she compares him; certainly Ackerley does not blame his sexual problem, which is not homosexuality but his failure to achieve a satisfactory sexual relationship, on his mother, his religion, or his country.

But what is particularly interesting in a study of Isherwood is the striking similarity between Ackerley's words and those of

[11]

an English homosexual earlier pictured by Isherwood in *Down There on a Visit.* Here is Ackerley:

I was now on the sexual map and proud of my place on it. I did not care for the word "homosexual" or any label, but I stood among the men, not among the women. Girls I despised; vain, silly creatures, how could their smooth, soft, bulbous bodies compare in attraction with the muscular beauty of men? Their place was the harem, from which they should never have been released: true love, equal and understanding love, occurred only between men. I saw myself in the tradition of the Classic Greeks.

And here is Isherwood's character Ambrose speaking (from a Greek island, incidentally):

"What most people don't realize is that, when we take over, women will be much better off, actually, than they are now. They'll be beautifully looked after on the breeding farms, as wards of the State. And, surely, most of them would greatly prefer artificial insemination, anyway? It's quite obvious that they have no real interest in men—beyond wanting to order them about—and that's why they have no taste whatsoever when it comes to picking attractive ones. They just don't know men's points; they've no eye for them. Women are all Lesbians, really—they take naturally to all that ineffectual feminine messing about—cuddling and petting—the kind of thing Ingres shows so brilliantly in that Turkish bath painting of his—though, I must say, I never could look at it without a shudder of cold horror."

Edward, the homosexual in Isherwood's second novel, *The Memorial*, is a more conventional figure; he has "survived" the war less successfully than his friend who died in it. At the end Edward, pursuing his ghostlike existence, discovers that the latest of his boys thinks of war as a historical event of which he dimly remembers hearing his elders speak. Bound in a strange sort of alliance with a woman who loves him but who must find her sexual adventures with young men, Edward is a failed suicide (gun in mouth, but the bullet failed to kill) doomed to be deserted by one of his boy-lovers after the other, and to return always to Margaret, the threatening-comforting mother figure, infinitely kind.

[12]

In "On Reugan Island," from *Goodbye to Berlin*, the homosexual is Peter, the weakling Englishman with vague, neuras-
thenic ailments all beyond the reach of any known form of
psychotherapy; they have all been tried. Peter is infatuated
with Otto Nowak, the German working-class boy whose
whole family is so brilliantly portrayed by Isherwood in the
following section of *Goodbye to Berlin*. Otto deserts Peter,
who resents the boy's heterosexual encounters, and Peter re-
turns to England and to nothingness. All of Isherwood's homosexual lovers are deserted by the boys they adore—it is as
inevitable as aging. The exploitive, repetitive, constantly failing quality of these homosexual relationships seems to en-
lighten, in Isherwood's work, the futility of most passionate,
driven attachments. The only characters in Isherwood's novels
with any capacity for love are women.

The futility of the homosexual affair as Isherwood has portrayed it lies not primarily in its sterility (the production of
children is not, for Isherwood, a necessary sign of life affirma-
tion, though the proper treatment of them is) but in the degree
to which it is threatened, uncertain, life-denying. Most of
Isherwood's homosexuals die metaphorical deaths. Furthermore, the futility of homosexual relationships is associated,
though never blatantly, with the destruction of hope, in the
early books with Nazism and war, in the later books with the
impermanence of love in modern society. The "camp" homosexual Quakers in *The World in the Evening* annoy, amuse,
and disturb in equal degrees as they attempt to fit their lives
into American Quakerdom, and Stephen Monk's affair with
the homosexual Michael, his first marital infidelity, carries
implications of Monk's failure to confront life.

A Single Man is a triumphant use of the homosexual theme.
A comic masterpiece, it derives not only marvelous humor
from the homosexuality of its chief character but a superbly

[13]

unobtrusive metaphor for the futility of all sensual human attachments. Set in California, it brings Isherwood around to a consideration of the American attitude toward homosexuality and all sexual guilt. His perception of America's hysterical reaction to, and fascination with, homosexuality long precedes, however, his first visit to the United States. In 1933, "Chris" and a friend have gone on a tour of Berlin dives (in *Goodbye to Berlin*):

The Salomé turned out to be very expensive and even more depressing than I had imagined. A few stage lesbians and some young men with plucked eyebrows lounged at the bar, uttering occasional raucous guffaws or treble hoots—supposed, apparently, to represent the laughter of the damned. The whole premises are painted gold and inferno-red—crimson plush inches thick, and vast gilded mirrors. It was pretty full. The audience consisted chiefly of respectable middle-aged tradesmen and their families, exclaiming in good-humored amazement: "Do they really?" and "Well, I never!" We went out half-way through the cabaret performance, after a young man in a spangled crinoline and jewelled breast-caps had painfully but successfully executed three splits.

At the entrance we met a party of American youths, very drunk, wondering whether to go in. Their leader was a small stocky young man in pince-nez, with an annoyingly prominent jaw.

"Say," he asked Fritz, "what's on here?"

"Men dressed as women," Fritz grinned.

The little American simply couldn't believe it. "Men dressed as *women*? As *women*, hey? Do you mean they're *queer*?"

"Eventually we're all queer," drawled Fritz solemnly, in lugubrious tones. . . .

"You *queer*, too, hey?" demanded the little American, turning suddenly on me.

"Yes," I said, "very queer indeed."

He stood before me a moment, panting, thrusting out his jaw, uncertain, it seemed, whether he ought not to hit me in the face. Then he turned, uttered some kind of wild college battle-cry, and, followed by the others, rushed headlong into the building.

In Isherwood's latest novel, a married man, given to occasional homosexual passions, frees himself from his most recent attachment and urges the boy not to consider impossible the love of a girl. Homosexuality in Isherwood's work is neither sneered at nor glorified, and he expressed this attitude years before fashion sanctioned it.

In a consideration of Isherwood's major work, a division clearly suggests itself: Documentaries and Novels. I call "documentaries" those works in which "Christopher Isherwood," the ventriloquist's dummy, appears; "novels," those works in which he does not. The documentaries are: *The Last of Mr. Norris, Lions and Shadows, Journey to a War, Goodbye to Berlin, Prater Violet, The Condor and the Cows,* and *Down There on a Visit.* The novels are: *All the Conspirators, The Memorial, The World in the Evening, A Single Man,* and *A Meeting by the River.* The division is less arbitrary, or superficial, than may at first appear. If, for example, we call the books with the "Christopher Isherwood" narrator "political," we begin to see that it is precisely in the use of this particular device of point of view that Isherwood's success as a political novelist lies. Even his so-called factual books, *Lions and Shadows, Journey to a War, The Condor and the Cows,* are documentaries in their presentation of events, in their selection of incident, and in the character of the dummy who tells the story. In all of these, emotion has been transposed or dissolved, and the distance which political novels require has been achieved. An interesting comparison occurs with Orwell. Certainly it can be argued that Orwell's best, most perceptive, and most moving works are his nonfiction: *Homage to Catalonia, The Road to Wigan Pier,* and many of the short essays. When, however, Orwell comes to write novels, the same genius does not manifest itself, and in his last two novels, *Animal Farm* and *1984,* the powerful emotion infusing the works pushes them too far in the direction of polemics or frenzied prophecy. What Isherwood has achieved in his docu-

[15]

mentaries is the quality of Orwell's nonfiction, but presented, not personally, but through the eyes of an observing, not emotionally committed narrator. This is not to suggest that a comparison between Orwell and Isherwood should be pushed too far; Isherwood was apparently unable to create his documentaries while his emotions were still engaged, and his works therefore lack the sense of political courage and special acumen which mark Orwell's nonfictional achievement. Orwell, furthermore, was the most committed of men, full of wrathful scorn for those who advocate "non-violence behind the guns of the American Navy," while Isherwood looked, with more prescience but less immediacy, to an age which must be pacifist or die.

Two introductory questions emerge upon consideration of Isherwood's documentaries: how close are these works to actual fact, and what are we to make of the character of "Christopher Isherwood," the ventriloquist's dummy?

V. S. Pritchett has written of Isherwood that his "career represents the interaction of the reporter and the artist at its most delicate balance." The characters in the documentaries are closely modeled on actual people, and Isherwood is proud of the fact that "it's all quite historically correct. I took great trouble, indeed I always do, with the historical aspects, the setting and the details. I like to get all that right." He has spoken of the diaries he has always kept extensively, "and they give me a sense of security because I feel at least this part is factual. Having, however, built on these little islands of fact, I think one goes back and reconstructs everything and changes everything and interferes with everything. But I do find it a great reassurance—the only kind of reassurance one can have—to have had some notes of an actual experience or an actual scene or people or whatever."

[16]

Be that as it may, a comparison of Isherwood's portrayals of characters in his documentaries, and his "factual" portraits of actual people, reveals immediately the particular and peculiar art of the documentary. His factual portraits of Ernst Toller, Virginia Woolf, and Klaus Mann, published in *Exhumations*, and his sketch of Aldous Huxley, reprinted in the Aldous Huxley memorial volume, are lifeless and unevocative. Without the dummy, without the touch of the artist, Isherwood is strangely feeble. The reporter without the artist is only a competent journalist. If we examine closely statements about W. H. Auden from the documentaries and from interviews or articles, the distinction—subtle but palpable—is demonstrated.

Here Isherwood speaks to an interviewer of the trip he and Auden made to war-torn China in 1938: "We couldn't help thinking of ourselves as somewhat absurd, especially since Auden through hell and high water wore carpet slippers because of his corns."

Here is a passage from *Journey to a War*, the book which resulted from the Chinese journey:

I slept uneasily that night—in my trousers and shirt: not wishing to have to leave the train and bolt for cover in my pajamas. Auden, with his monumental calm, had completely undressed.

Also:

While we were at the front this morning our guide said: "Over there are the lines to which we shall retreat." "But you *mustn't* retreat," Auden interjected, in spite of himself, rather severely.

It is the voice of the speaker, and his implicit characterization, his constant presence, which brings art to reportage. Again, here is Isherwood in a factual article entitled "Some Notes on Auden's Early Poetry":

Auden is essentially a scientist: perhaps I should say "a schoolboy

[17]

scientist." He has, that is to say, the scientific training and the scientific interests of a very intelligent schoolboy. He has covered the groundwork, but doesn't propose to go any further.

And here is schoolboy Auden in *Lion and Shadows:*

His ambition was to become a mining engineer; and his playbox was full of thick scientific books on geology and metals and machines, borrowed from his father's library. . . . With his hinted forbidden knowledge and stock of mispronounced scientific words, portentously uttered, he enjoyed among us, his semi-savage credulous school fellows, the status of a kind of witch-doctor.

The rare gift of touching a portrait with life is discovered by Isherwood only in the documentaries; the lifelessness of his actual portraits attests to this. "It is usually easy to describe strangers," Isherwood writes in his obituary essay on Virginia Woolf. "Yet, although I didn't meet Virginia more than half-a-dozen times, I find it nearly impossible to write anything about her which will carry the breath of life." But there is not a stranger in Berlin, London, Los Angeles, China, South America into whom "Christopher Isherwood" does not breathe life. The dummy holds the secret.

"The first person singular of the German stories, Herr Christoph, or Herr Issyvoo, is the most persuasive of literary salesmen," Cyril Connolly has written. "He is persuasive because he is so insinuatingly bland and anonymous, nothing rouses him, nothing shocks him. While secretly despising us he could not at the same time be more tolerant; his manners are charming and he is somehow on our side against the characters." We do not really need Stephen Spender's memories of Berlin—"Christopher, so far from being the self-effacing spectator he depicts in his novels, was really the center of his characters and neither could they exist without him nor he without them"—to understand the extraordinary transformation from fact to art. "Day after day," Spender continues, "against the background of pine trees, lakes or streets, I witnessed that transformation taking place in his mind, where the real becomes malleable, the people who are garrulous and shabby in life become the crystal entertainers of fiction."

The whole question of point of view and the reliability of the narrator has been seen as central in modern studies of the novel. It is the more extraordinary, therefore, that critics have failed to recognize that Isherwood alone developed the form of the documentary and the particular narrator who makes it possible. Not even Wayne Booth, whose *Rhetoric of Fiction* is devoted to the relationship between the chosen point of narration and the sense of truth and morality conveyed by the story, has seen how Isherwood's first-person dummy makes possible a kind of veracity that is freed from an intrusive sense of morality or ideological bias. Yet a study of Isherwood's fictional technique makes clear the apparent anomaly that political novels are best narrated by a first-person viewer of bland personality, while interior novels of sensibility are, as Henry James of course discovered, impossible successfully to render in the first person. Furthermore, the bland first-person narrator saves the political novel from too strident a presentation of ideology so that, in the end, the moral point of view for which Wayne Booth hankers is, in fact, created.

Apparently it did not at first occur to Isherwood to call his new-style narrator candidly by his own name; one assumes that the use of his middle names, William Bradshaw, in *The Last of Mr. Norris* indicates an attempt at some mild form of disguise, the same sort he was later to wrap around the characters in *Lions and Shadows:* Hugh Weston is Auden, Stephen Savage is Spender, Cheuret is André Mangeot, Philip Lindley is Hector Wintle. By the time of the publication of *The Last of Mr. Norris,* however, William Bradshaw would certainly have come home one evening to find Christopher

Isherwood asleep in his bed, and the mild disguise was abandoned.

Mr. Norris, together with all the other Berlin characters, was originally intended to form part of a "huge episodic novel" entitled *The Lost*. There is surely little to regret in the abandonment of that huge production, although John Lehmann, whose magazine *New Writing* provided perhaps the only possible outlet for the stories which eventually made up *Goodbye to Berlin*, spoke sadly of "these fragments." Lehmann was one of the first to recognize Isherwood as wholly revolutionary in reconciling the "claims of the artist and the claims of the moralist"; he had neither turned away from fascist-menaced Europe nor been deflected by the sight of it into "more obviously propagandist and political activities." Yet Lehmann did not perceive that "these fragments" were, in fact, hardly as unordered as their self-abnegating author chose to claim. What Isherwood referred to in 1938 as "this short loosely-connected sequence of diaries and sketches" came, not surprisingly, to be accepted as exactly that by its readers. Thus in 1960 Stanley Poss in an interview all but apologizes to Isherwood for finding a "kind of contrapuntal organization (if you'll forgive such a pretentious term) in *Goodbye to Berlin*":

For example [he continues] the six parts seem to me to be played off against one another. The first diary section, "Autumn 1930," could be juxtaposed, let's say, deliberately, with the last diary section '32–'33. And then, "Sally Bowles" and "On Ruegen Island" seem to me to be in a way halves, that is, kind of polarities of one another; and "The Nowaks" and "The Landauers" certainly seem to be related.

Indeed, the episodes were constructed around the disintegration and dehumanization of a modern city where, as in Conrad's *The Secret Agent*, the criminals and the police operate by the same convictions. "Christopher Isherwood," who refuses to judge the characters, who, indeed, allows himself to be charmed by them, provides the perfect unity: the focused, the unjudging camera, which visualizes but does not preach. Isherwood is fond of referring to some of his works as dynamic portraits; it is in the dynamic portraits, with the dummy as the focal point, that Isherwood, like Conrad with Marlow, gains for himself the obviously essential aesthetic distance. Distance, of time as well as of narrator, is essential to Isherwood, as Lehmann does not appear to understand. "What treasures there would have been for us to lighten the darkest day," he wrote about the war period, "if the creator of the Nowaks and Mr. Norris had cast his compassionate and humorous eye upon the ardent follies of our wartime scene." But Isherwood's "compassionate and humorous eye" required the passage of twenty years before its visions of England on the verge of war could be published. This distance came to be called "heartlessness" by many, including Isherwood himself when he spoke of *The Last of Mr. Norris*, but that word is as inexact, as misleading as the comments frequently made upon his two masters, Forster and Ibsen: of the first, that he is never wholly serious; of the second, that he is serious only in a social context. All three, eschewing propaganda and ready judgment, discover art.

"Christopher Isherwood," however, is not, strictly speaking, a camera. He is more a mirror in which everyone sees his own fantasies: the homosexual, that Chris will understand; the promiscuous Sally Bowles, that Chris may be abused and used, conveniently cast in the role of "father" to a baby abortion has freed her of. Chris is the only possible confidant to the rich and cultured Jew who will not make the effort to escape the Nazis; the only possible lover, though only for an afternoon, for the strange sick girl in the TB sanitarium:

[21]

My mouth pressed against Erna's hot, dry lips. I had no particular sensation of contact: all this was part of the long, rather sinister symbolic dream which I seem to have been dreaming throughout the day. "I'm so happy, this evening . . ." Erna whispered.

He is the apologist for the many people like Fräulein Schroeder, his landlady, who "are acclimatizing themselves. After all, whatever government is in power, they are doomed to live in this town."

The dummy, perfectly developed in *Goodbye to Berlin*, was conveniently ready to hand for the "autobiography," *Lions and Shadows*. Isherwood was prepared to regard the England of his pre-Berlin days with an eye, and a narrator "I," Christopher Isherwood—both trained in the streets and homes of Hitler's Berlin. In a notice to the reader at the beginning of the book, Isherwood, in his by now accustomed bland tones, declares what the book is not: it contains no revelations, is never indiscreet, and is not even entirely true. Although *Lions and Shadows* is subtitled "the education of a novelist," it is not really that. Far from revealing to us how Isherwood became the novelist he is, the book instead shows us the England of his youth, revealed through the eye of the mature writer whose origins remain obscure. Indeed, the character of Allen Chalmers in the book—the novelist Edward Upward, whose identity has only recently been revealed—might lay greater claim to *Lions and Shadows* as the account of *his* education. It was he, not Isherwood, who was to write out the Montmere story, he who was to find in Marxism the solution to his generation's political problems, he who was to continue to battle the establishment. Isherwood, on the other hand, was content to picture his generation (not including himself) simply as they were. It is doubtful, therefore, if Auden has ever been presented more marvelously, or if any biography of that poet will ever be able to ignore Isherwood's portrait of the boy "Wystan":

I see him boxing, with his ferocious frown, against a boy twice his size; I see him frowning as he sings opposite me in the choir, surpliced, in an enormous Eton collar, above which his great red flaps of ears stand out, on either side of his narrow scowling pudding-white face. In our dormitory religious arguments, which were frequent, I hear him heatedly exclaiming against churches in which the cross was merely painted on the wall behind the altar: they ought, he said, to be burnt down and their vicars put into prison. His people, we gathered, were high Anglican.

"Christopher Isherwood," throughout *Lions and Shadows*, is seen as immature, passive, always admiring some stronger, more forceful or attractive figure. In fact, as Stephen Spender's and John Lehmann's autobiographies indicate, Isherwood was a markedly active and dominating figure among his friends; if he did not like a line of poetry, Auden immediately crossed it out. The dummy has been formed to serve its particular purpose in this masterful book in the documentary form.

Not until *Prater Violet* appeared in 1945 did Isherwood use the form so successfully again. The seven intervening years contained his spiritual crisis and the discovery of California as his home. The minor documentary, *Journey to a War*, written in collaboration with W. H. Auden, appeared the year after *Lions and Shadows*. Isherwood had also collaborated with Auden on three plays: *The Dog Beneath the Skin* (1935), *The Ascent of F6* (1936), and *On the Frontier* (1938). These require no special attention here. They are almost always discussed, perhaps with veracity, as though Auden alone had written them. Isherwood told George Wickes in 1965:

Auden had already written some verse plays before we collaborated. He wrote a very short play called *Paid on Both Sides*, which comes in his first book of poems. Then he wrote a play called *The Dance of Death* for a theatrical group headed by Rupert Doone, who was later our director; I think we may have even discussed a little how he should do this, but we certainly didn't collaborate. We sort of eased into collaboration. You see, we were very intimate friends all this time. . . .

He would come out and visit with me wherever I was. For instance, we did the final collaboration on *The Dog Beneath the Skin* in Copenhagen. We wrote *The Ascent of F6* mostly in Cintra, outside Lisbon. As for *On the Frontier*, that was written all over the place, partly on a very slow old boat called *The Empress of Asia* coming back from China between Japan and Vancouver. We worked wherever we were together. The whole collaboration really amounted to this: here was Auden, who was obviously a major poet, and all I felt I was doing was perhaps providing a slightly firmer framework on which these poems could be presented. I don't mean that Auden was incapable of dramaturgy because as a matter of fact he did a great many of the scenes. But my real function was very much that of a librettist, and he was the composer.

Suffice it to say that it is the poems Auden wrote for the plays that will last, not the "slightly firmer framework." Even allowing for Isherwood's inevitable modesty, it is difficult to discover any overwhelmingly Isherwoodian ideas in the plays, except, of course, that of "The Test," which was to keep cropping up in Isherwood's works for a long while.

Journey to a War is a different matter. Isherwood, characteristically, takes as little credit as possible:

. . . we did in fact take turns keeping the diary. . . . One day Auden would do it, the next day I would do it. But it had to be done with an overall style. So I just took the entire diary and wrote the prose narrative. And when I prepared the text I tried to credit Auden with any bright remarks which he had made during the day.

The prose narrative is his work, and a good job too. The dummy "Christopher Isherwood" is off with his friend Auden to see the battles in China. They are both Forsterian characters, as befits the dedication, and remarkably like Philip and Caroline Abbott in the midst of the flying vegetables at the Italian Opera. Here too babies are murdered, and one wonders if Isherwood was thinking of *Where Angels Fear to Tread* when he described an evening at a Chinese play:

The theatre was packed. Everyone in the audience was laughing, talking, shouting across the auditorium to greet his friends. People kept coming in and going out. Attendants ran round with hot face-towels and glasses of tea. It seemed nearly impossible to hear a single word from the stage: but no doubt this didn't matter, because the public knew the whole play by heart. As Auden remarked, it was like hearing Mass in an Italian church.

"Christopher Isherwood" sits, with Auden, drinking Chinese gin of terrific strength and, drunk and drenched to the skin, sets out on horseback for the battlefront. "We shouted to each other, sang and joked. Later, turning maudlin, I sentimentally embraced my horse and told it, in German, the story of my life." It is to be noticed that Isherwood, not yet consciously on the path to sainthood, now sees the dummy as an almost Dostoevskian fool.

In the six years between *Journey to a War* and *Prater Violet*, Isherwood published little. These were the years of his dark night of the soul, though one cannot imagine him using so pretentious sounding a phrase; pretentious sounding or not, it appears to be accurate. Apart from reviewing books and writing the brief obituary essay on Virginia Woolf, he produced two stories, both published in the *New Yorker*. "I Am Waiting," a mildly supernatural story of an old man who finds himself undergoing certain psychic experiences, was published in 1939; the *New Yorker* changed the setting from England to Connecticut because such a story set in England at that time seemed to them unfeeling. The other story, "Take It or Leave It," appeared in the *New Yorker* three years later. It was written "chiefly to please my friend René Blanc-Roos. . . . A warm but severe admirer of my work, he ordered me to write something, anything; he was determined that I should keep myself in condition." René Blanc-Roos was a language instructor and wrestling coach at Haverford College when Isherwood was doing wartime service with the Quakers in Pennsylvania; in gratitude, Isherwood later dedicated *Prater Violet* to him. For the next three years Isherwood published only material for the Vedanta Society of Southern California, which he had joined. John Lehmann, in his magazine the *Penguin New Writing*, printed a record of one of the early religious groups; "The Day at La Verne" is an undistinguished account which Isherwood wisely did not include in *Exhumations;* it is most interesting as a description of a precursor of like groups which were soon to spring up in California and elsewhere.

Prater Violet is a brilliant novella which re-creates the whole lunatic process involved in the making of a successful film. Isherwood, in fact, had been working on the writing of films for many years prior to 1945, but "Christopher Isherwood" of the story assumes no expertise as he trails after the director in England during the early thirties. Indeed, the dummy is depicted here rather more harshly than before, complete with mother and brother who are amiable and long-suffering in the presence of arrogant, German-speaking Chris. In later years Isherwood was to say that *Prater Violet* had provided the best use of the character "Christopher Isherwood," because in Bergmann, the German movie director, he "was up against a real talker." Bergmann, like all Isherwood's characters in the documentaries, was based on a real person, the film director Berthold Viertel. He, discussing *Prater Violet* in *Theater Arts* shortly after the book appeared, seemed somehow less real than Isherwood's creation of him. As Spender has observed, Isherwood's characters do not exist without him.

Prater Violet differs from the earlier documentaries in the amount of emotion which is permitted to the dummy; here he, and not alone those he observes, suffers. When, at the end of the book, "Christopher Isherwood" leaves Bergmann to walk home, he ruminates desperately on his own despair. He considers, since *Prater Violet* was written after Isherwood's conversion to Vedanta, that other way, which would mean "that I should no longer be a person. I should no longer be Christopher Isherwood." "That," he continues, "I could never face." Critics, indulging, as is their unfortunate wont, in biographical criticism, suggested that this final scene of desperation refuted Isherwood's supposed peace found in Vedanta. But Isherwood was not, in 1945, writing his current spiritual state into the novel; as the most gifted of the artist-reporters, he was re-creating the general state of mind of the prewar years. All of *Prater Violet* is a dazzling, miniature portrait of the times: the escapism of a silly film set against the hell-bound rush of Europe. At the end of the film-making, the highly successful movie *Prater Violet* has earned its director a job in Hollywood, escape from the Nazis and from art. "You know," Bergmann says to Chris in the book, "I feel absolutely no shame before you. We are like married men who meet in a whorehouse." Isherwood is the only writer who could set down that sentence and leave it alone.

When an interviewer seemed to suggest that in the fifteen years following *Goodbye to Berlin* Isherwood had, as a reviewer had suggested, produced little beside *Prater Violet*, Isherwood probably came as close to asperity as is possible for him. "People," he said, "get a wonderful view of my lack of production by blissfully ignoring two-thirds of my work. I *only* produced, I don't know, what was it—three, four books related to Vedanta in one way or another. And then, of course, there was this travel book, *The Condor and the Cows*, which I now see as one of my best books."

Few would agree with him. Yet the book is readable, and remarkable in its evocation of South America. The book can be seen as transitional, as though Isherwood were looking forward to other works as well as at the scenery. Anticipating *A Single Man,* for example, the traveling dummy is allowed to see his body as distinct from "I."

The long-suffering body, which must somehow adapt itself to all its master's whims and wanderings, shivers suddenly and wants a coat. The lungs breathe the thinning air and the nerves send out their first signals of uneasiness. The muscles, so long relaxed in the sweating heat of the plains, begin to tighten and ache.

For the most part, however, "Christopher" is still playing the fool, embarrassed to receive a South American author's essays presented in person—"As usual, I was humiliated, having nothing to return. Auden would have sat down and dashed them off a couple of sonnets."

A week after one has read the book, most of the impressions of South America have vanished; what remains is "Christopher Isherwood" performing, re-creating his characters, even giving us the chance to see the dummy playing the dummy:

We share a table with a married couple from New York. . . .
They have been married about ten years, have children, seem happy. This is their first long trip alone together since their honeymoon. It was, almost certainly, her idea. He's a little unwilling. He can't quite relax. For him, as for so many Americans of his kind, a pleasure journey is just another sort of investment—a sound one, most likely, but he has got to watch it. With his puzzled collegiate frown, he is perpetually trying to assess the whole undertaking in terms of value and service. . . . She is equally determined—to enjoy herself and to make him enjoy himself too. The energy which she brings to this task is really beautiful and touching. . . .
Perhaps even she isn't quite consciously aware of the significance of their trip. A holiday of this kind is the test, and may be the vindication, of an entire relationship. After years of accepted routine—office work, raising children, shopping, cooking—you take your marriage out of its little suburban frame and set it against a tremendous classic background of ocean, mountains and stars. How does it stand up? Is it self-sufficient, deep, brilliant and compact as a Vermeer? Or a messy amateur sketch which doesn't compose?

[28]

What can we do to help them? We have our place, of course, in the scheme of travel values. We belong to that necessary class of Some Interesting People We Met on the Boat. We are like The Ruins and The Little Restaurant with Atmosphere. No journey is complete without us. We shall be discussed and described to relatives and friends at home.

Our duty, therefore, is to be strange. Not alarmingly odd; that would scare them. Not enviably independent; that might make them feel somehow dissatisfied with the limitations of their own lives. I must tell stories about China, England, Germany, Hollywood; about Nazis, missionaries and movie stars. I must appear bohemian, lively, happy-go-lucky. But I must also drop reassuring hints of wander-weariness, of a longing to settle down in a home of my own. And I must make it very clear, especially to him, that I really earn and respect money.

Isherwood announced that *Down There on a Visit* would probably be the last appearance of the ventriloquist's dummy, or "that thing," as he calls him, because "this fictional Christopher Isherwood got absolutely too big for his britches and became rather unmanageable." Isherwood had, in fact, excluded a drug-taking scene originally intended for *Down There on a Visit* from that book because it was "almost exclusively about Chris and his experiences," and did not belong in the story. (The scene is published in *Exhumations*.) As Isherwood's interest clearly shifted from exclusive focus on the objects of Chris's attention to Chris himself, he had to guard against slipping from the documentary into the novel form. By the time the last documentary, *Down There on a Visit*, had appeared, Isherwood had already published *The World in the Evening*, his first "novel" in over twenty years, and was, perhaps, beginning to perceive that this form rather than the documentary would become the necessary mode for him.

Down There on a Visit was published in 1962; one section had already appeared in 1959. By this time, Isherwood was sufficiently distant from the sufferings of the war years to be able to perceive them from the vantage point of the dummy. In addition, the spiritual struggle with Vedanta and the characters in that struggle, including Gerald Heard, could now be re-created in documentary form. Accounts of hell can only be written by those who have achieved the return journey. When Isherwood began to work on *A Single Man*, published two years later than *Down There on a Visit*, he tried to write it as another documentary with "Christopher Isherwood," but had to abandon this approach; by now, he realized, his work had to be in the straight novel form.

For "Christopher Isherwood," as can be seen in all the documentaries after *Goodbye to Berlin*, had become less a camera, or mirror, and more himself the object of the author's discerning eye, But, regarding the dummy, Isherwood was not as gentle as the dummy had been with the objects of *his* perception. In *Prater Violet*, for example, "Christopher Isherwood," whose creator is now writing the autobiography not only of a doomed age but of a growing spiritual despair, is seen, from time to time, quite as though he were as morally fatuous as Sally Bowles:

"Cousin Edith's dentist," said my mother, as she passed me a teacup, "seems to be quite convinced Hitler's going to invade Austria soon."
"Oh, indeed?" I took a big sip of tea and sat back, feeling suddenly in a very good humor. "Well, no doubt the *dental* profession has sources of information denied to the rest of us. But I must say, in my ignorance, I entirely fail to see how . . ."
I was off. My mother poured fresh cups of tea for Richard and herself. They exchanged milk and sugar with smiling pantomime and settled back comfortably in their chairs, like people in a restaurant when the orchestra strikes up a tune which everybody knows by heart.
Within ten minutes, I had set up and knocked down every argument the dentist could possibly have been expected to produce, and many that he couldn't. I used a lot of my favorite words:

Gauleiter, solidarity, démarche, dialectic, Gleichschaltung, infiltration, Anchluss, realism, tranche, cadre. Then, after pausing to light another cigarette and get my breath, I started to sketch, none too briefly, the history of National Socialism since the Munich Putsch.

Chris, getting too big for his britches, has become a camera with a self-timer attached.

In *Down There on a Visit* the narrator is frankly double: an older Chris watches the younger Chris who he feels is sometimes his father, sometimes his son. Certainly Chris's reactions are as interesting, and usually more significant, than those of the other characters. Chris is seen in four separate scenes: "Mr. Lancaster," an account of Chris's first trip to Germany when he was twenty-three; "Ambrose," the weakest of the sections, in which Chris is again mainly the observer, and one learns, except for the information that a man can have sexual intercourse with a chicken, little that is new or startling; "Waldemar," an account of England in 1938 and Chris's departure for America; and "Paul," a Hollywood story of a highly successful professional lover who, achieving the abyss, reveals Chris as a dabbler in life's sufferings. Paul is used brilliantly as a foil for Chris on his spiritual journey, forcing him to examine his pretenses and to remain, at the end, quite outside the hell he has watched the other characters experience; he has only been down there on a visit.

Down There on a Visit, particularly in its two best sections, "Waldemar" and "Paul," is a brilliant example of how suffering (or, as we say, life) can be transmuted into art. Because Isherwood has given us, in his pamphlet *An Approach to Vedanta*, certain facts about his early days in the United States, we are able to compare these with the account in *Down There on a Visit*. What is important here is not *how* the transformation took place; that is not open to understanding. It is the

[31]

extent and subtlety of the transformation that intrigues us. Isherwood has managed, astonishingly, to keep separate "the man who suffers and the mind which creates." The impression of the study of Yoga derived from Isherwood's pamphlets written for the Vedanta society, for example, differs radically from the re-creation of Chris's studies and efforts in *Down There on a Visit*. George Wickes asked Isherwood if being a Vedantist hadn't affected the sort of writing he did. Isherwood's answer is profound, and ought to be translated from its Hindu terms into words all those who like to rush back and forth between the life and the work of any author could readily accept:

What you always have to remember about the Hindu concept of life is this very important thing which they call *dharma*, which is your individual duty based upon your talents, capacities, and potentialities as of that particular moment. And there's such a thing as having the *dharma* of being an artist . . . and in the context of this *dharma*, it's your duty and indeed the only way toward spiritual development to do your very best along those particular lines. This again of course is not at all exclusively a Hindu idea. It comes in the parable of the talents of Jesus of Nazareth.

When *Down There on a Visit* was finished, it must have become clear to Isherwood that what his *dharma* as an artist required of him were novels—wholly formed, created works, not written in the documentary mode with the reflecting first-person narrator which he had discovered, developed, and perfected. Each novel must find its own necessary form. He had already written a "novel" in *The World in the Evening* (1954).

Yet one cannot go on to discuss the "novels," as opposed to the documentaries, without pointing to the extraordinary accomplishment of this last of the documentaries. The four sections of *Down There on a Visit*, although uneven, do precisely and uniquely reveal the four versions of hell which modern man has most consistently chosen to explore. The book, as Stuart Hampshire has written, shocks because Isherwood is truthful in an unfamiliar way: the shock is stunning. True, when the narrator becomes, not alone the mirror for doomed worlds, but also the mirror of his own perverted strivings, we have the uncomfortable sense of encountering Steppenwolf in a novel by Scott Fitzgerald. Nevertheless, in the end we are grateful, in Hampshire's words, that "there are no reassuring hammerblows, as in Orwell, which tell the reader quite unmistakably which side he ought to be on, leaving him complacent among the angels." The dummy "Christopher Isherwood" has visited every hell except that of complacency. Immensely readable, as always, one of the most fascinating and accurate record of several eras, *Down There on a Visit* is perhaps the best of Isherwood's documentaries, because it took the most courage to write. It is clearly the best work of fiction we have on the spiritual odyssey of his generation.

Isherwood began his first novel, before the documentary form had presented itself to him, when he was twenty-one years old. It was published when he was twenty-three and, until he became better known, sold very few copies. *All the Conspirators* (1928), as Isherwood has pointed out, was burdened with a Shakespearean title too fancy for a novel bearing no possible connection with *Julius Caesar*, and contained not altogether clear passages as well as some echoes and reminiscences of Forster, Joyce, and Woolf. What is remarkable about the book is its accomplished technique, style, and tone: Isherwood might not have discovered his true voice, but he was clearly a born writer, and his novel is still in print. Cyril Connolly, while overpraising the book in later years, called it mature, readable, concentrated, and perceptive; it was all of these despite its author's early age, and, despite Isherwood's youthful fascination with private worlds, it is an available book, not only to another generation of "angry young men," but also to readers the same age as the novel itself, or older. The story is of a young man possessed, not untypically, with more creative energy than creative talent; he is, in any case, not allowed to live his own life, but is destroyed by his dominating mother in the most "tea-table" possible way. His sister, driven to marry a Charles Wilcox sort of character, shares her brother's sacrificial destiny: they are the sacrificed. As Isherwood himself has pointed out, while the present generation of youth struggles against society, institutions, and the centers of social power, his generation saw the family as the villains; their revolution was always against the filial virtues and was rarely successful.

The sister, Joan, in *All the Conspirators* shows certain tendencies to crack, if not to break, the mold for young ladies in novels, and it is worth mentioning at the start of a discussion of Isherwood's "novels" that in these works, as opposed to the documentaries, women are created as characters. This is an unusual accomplishment in a male writer of novels in the fifties and sixties, if not earlier, and it has been largely ignored by the reviewers. John Wain, for example, in reviewing *The World in the Evening*, seems to find the portrait of the woman novelist extraordinary because of its resemblance to Katherine Mansfield, rather than—a harder achievement—because of its resemblance to a human being. The women in the documentaries are all stereotypes; individual characterization is not the hallmark of documentaries. It is perhaps the expectation of stereotypes in Isherwood's novels which encourages all reviewers to see the women there as stereotypes, chiefly as "mother figures."

[34]

Whether or not Isherwood himself has felt some sort of struggle with a "mother figure," it is clear that his reviewers think he has, and they pay more attention to what they hear of him than to his books; they have, in any case, continued to remark on the flight from the mother as a central theme in his novels. Yet since *All the Conspirators*, where the hero is indeed in flight from a villainous mother, "mother figures" do not seem in special abundance. True, Isherwood dedicates no book to his mother—and the dedications of Isherwood's books form a sort of minor autobiography. True, Isherwood's constant travels from the age of twenty-three away from his original home and finally toward a new one a continent and an ocean away may be indicative. Can one be sure, however, precisely of what they are indicative? To go from the life, known or hazarded, of a writer to his work is dangerous, occasionally fatal. Isherwood has suffered more this way than most.

The Memorial (1932) is a war novel—not about the fighting of war, but about what war has done to the survivors, only one of whom has actually been a soldier. The book is divided into four sections, each superficially independent as though it were a family photograph; as with family photographs, it is the changes from year to year which are most striking. The four parts—1928, 1920, 1925, 1929—are not presented in chronological order since stasis, not development, is what Isherwood is presenting. The technique has been compared, astonishingly, with Faulkner's *The Sound and the Fury*, a work Isherwood admits to never having read through. The comparison, however, is suggestive: if the two writers could not be more different in style, setting, tone, and theme, they are alike in evoking societies which have largely destroyed themselves. The Memorial of the title is a monument being unveiled to the war dead of an English town; the son of the "Hall" is among the dead, having left behind his father, wife, son, sister, friend,

[35]

all bereft by his absence and by the war which has spun them off from any evolving destiny, as a bit of a planet may be spun off into space. Here, as in all of Isherwood's novels, the relation between the private life and the public event is closer, more vital than it was in the novels of the previous generation. Yet differing from the documentaries, the novels allow the private individuals greater development, a more richly perceived interior life, a deeper intelligence. The most original character in *The Memorial* is Mary Scriven, *not* a mother figure despite the fact that she has a son. Mary Scriven, who will appear again in *The World in the Evening*, has reminded reviewers of the characters of Virginia Woolf—presumably because it is impossible to present the thoughts of a female character without seeming to imitate Mrs. Woolf.

In truth, it is the writings of Lytton Strachey which come most readily to mind in certain sections of *The Memorial*, such as the passage that follows, not because Strachey was an "influence," but because he shared with Isherwood the perception that public-school education and horrors like World War I were diabolically linked:

Eric was very, very sorry to hear that his father had been killed. The news added poignantly to his sense of desolation in the midst of the great school. It sharpened the misery of hearing the ugly jangling morning bell, of washing in cold water, of jostling downstairs to work. It seemed that his father's death was in some way connected with the school. That the school was responsible for it, as it was responsible for the bell, the water, and the work. The mornings were cold and raw, like reiterated sips of death. The dismal, untidy boot-room, the iron staircase, the bare dormitories, the stuffy little box of a study with the high weak electric light and thick blind which you got six for forgetting to draw—because of air-raids—and the soaked playing-fields and dusty class-rooms and icy-cold chapel—all seemed the atmosphere and scene of Death. For a week, Eric was almost intolerably miserable. Then he knew that he could bear it. It was no better, but he was stronger.

The World in the Evening (1954), Isherwood's next "novel," published more than twenty years after *The Memorial*, begins with Stephen Monk's flight from a Hollywood party and a Hollywood marriage and ends with his new-found ability, over cocktails with his now divorced but friendly second wife, to forgive himself. In between these two events lies the main body of the novel, Stephen Monk's recollections, while recovering from a smashed thigh, of his first marriage to a well-known woman novelist, Elizabeth Rydal, twelve years older than he. He recovers in the home of his Quaker guardian, a saintlike woman who had brought him up, and is nursed by a German refugee whose anxiety over her husband still in Europe is matched only by her total commitment to political action. *The World in the Evening* might be called the story of an odyssey from the evening world to the morning of the spirit.

Isherwood himself, like many of his contemporaries, underwent a spiritual odyssey in the years between *The Memorial* and *The World in the Evening*. It is nonetheless a mistake to equate his spiritual odyssey with that of the hero in the later novel, as Angus Wilson has done. Mr. Wilson feels that *The World in the Evening* fails because Isherwood could not create "an Alyosha, Myshkin or Bezuhov," and because Isherwood was probably "very little conscious of the triviality of Stephen's story." But the entire point about Stephen is his triviality, his embryonic quality. Mr. Wilson, furthermore, in his highly perceptive article on the novel, says mysteriously that "Mr. Isherwood has settled in post-war America, but the core of his imaginative life is still in pre-war Europe." Surely Mr. Isherwood's ability to portray America without satire, sneer, or sentimentality is one of his most notable characteristics. His are amongst the very few brilliant pictures of Hollywood; Fitzgerald and West alone rival him. The opening scene of *The World in the Evening* where Stephen Monk jealously pursues his wife to find her with a man in a doll's house—"two mating giants filling the dwarf world of the doll's house, and nearly bursting it apart with their heavings and writhings"— suggests that Isherwood's imaginative life now comprehends postwar America as well as prewar Europe. After *A Single Man* there could be no doubt of it.

It is Angus Wilson who points out that Isherwood, in *The World in the Evening*, explores for the first time "the complex patterns of emotional love." His readiness for this exploration perhaps persuaded him to return to the "novel" form; certainly his special achievement is to have created, in 1954, a novel in which the women characters are not, as in the novels of almost every other writer in the fifties (Angus Wilson himself is an exception), objects of the hero's scorn, leers, lusts, and aggressions, twice as simple as the hero, and five times as evil. The portraits of both Stephen's wives, the novelist and the sexpot, are "rounded," as Forster would say, that of the novelist extraordinarily so; both, as Mr. Wilson notices with astonishment, have a good deal that is unpleasant about them; they are, in short, successful creations. The need of the hero, in relation to them, to play a conventionally "feminine" role casts a rare new light on that role, and on the hero, who allows himself to be seduced by his homosexual lover as well.

When Stephen Monk, having finally achieved the passivity he desires by throwing himself in front of a truck, recalls his life with the novelist, Elizabeth Rydal, it is chiefly through the rereading of her letters to himself and others that her character is evoked. These letters reveal an astonishing ability, on Isherwood's part, to dramatize the actual problems and feelings a writer undergoes.

The letters, nonetheless, constitute the book's chief failure,

[38]

which is one of over-all technique. Isherwood apparently wrote the letters from Elizabeth Rydal with fatal ease. Many of them are beautifully done, and those to her friend Mary Scriven, at least, have a sort of acceptable probability. But all the other letters, and particularly that written by Stephen at the end of the book to his wife-of-the-doll-house, are little more than admissions of defeat. The difficulty, of course, is to get inside a character (the dummy had only to look, listen, and, later, respond) without the use of diaries, letters, or first-person narration: to show inner struggles without requiring that the characters expound them personally. This use of letters more seriously weakens Isherwood's most recent novel, *A Meeting by the River;* he has yet to master the rare technical skill of the novelist, to which James devoted his life, of being able to manifest in act, dialogue, and image the inner spiritual quality and growth of the characters.

Still, *The World in the Evening* is a remarkable achievement as a postwar *Bildungsroman:* the coming of age of a man who is of age. Beginning with legal and physical maturity, good looks, money, freedom, and some shreds of talent, this modern hero tries to discover value in a life whose value would hitherto have been taken for granted. He begins where the heroes of the *Bildungsroman,* young-men-from-the-provinces, and childhood-of-the-artist novels end. Endow your hero with everything, show him that life is the heavings and writhings of giants in the dwarf world of a doll's house, and bring him to the point where he is ready to start again. Stephen Monk is probably the first hero in modern literature whose problem is identical with that of Ibsen's heroines: he is not trying to "make it," but to live.

After the appearance of Somerset Maugham's *The Razor's Edge*—a book about which it was popularly said that Isherwood

[39]

modeled for the saint-hero Larry—Isherwood wrote an article entitled "The Problem of the Religious Novel." (It is reprinted in *Exhumations*.) His thesis was the difficulty of dramatizing the making of a saint. One may start, as Maugham does, with an ordinary enough young man. Suddenly, offstage as it were, something happens and the young man is transformed. But the actual conversion is the hardest of all inner states to show, partly because of the radical disconnection between the ordinary man and the saint, and partly because there is no factor of familiarity or self-recognition for the reader upon which the writer can rely. Probably the answer, which Isherwood might be reluctant to accept, is that saints make poor heroes because sainthood is beyond not only the abilities but also the desires of most men. Isherwood's biography of Ramakrishna, while not a novel, underlines the difficulty. There is no skill, though Isherwood makes a valiant attempt, which can render the quality of an Eastern avatar palpable to the as yet unconvinced Western mind. To a Westerner, for example, Ramakrishna's habit of going off into Samadji, a spiritual trancelike state, several times a day is disconcerting, if not ludicrous. Yet in this biography, as in his novels, Isherwood does perceive and present convincingly the connection between the saint and the fool.

Is *The World in the Evening* a novel about goodness or the making of a saint? Stephen Monk's name is suggestive, as are his orphaned state, his upbringing by a saintlike Quaker, and his almost incredible passivity before experience. Not until he bangs on the tin roof of the doll's house does he seem to take any action toward self-discovery. Yet he has had, all along, the saint's mysterious lack of self-identification, the weakness of self which can destroy or, in rare cases, exalt:

There was a night during the summer of 1937, at St Luc, when I'd

[40]

woken from heavy dreamless sleep after making love to Jane, and hadn't known who or where I was. I'd seemed to be looking down, from some impersonal no-place, at our two bodies lying in each other's arms on the bed. I could swear that I'd actually hesitated then, like a guest at the end of a party who looks at two overcoats not sure for a moment which is which, before I'd decided "that one's mine."

At the end of the book, however, he is only able to forgive himself; the height of maturity, but still prior, if just prior, to the beginning of sainthood. One senses that the novel is concerned principally with the life that may precede the possibility of sainthood.

It is little wonder that the reviewers, unable to fit the novelist, Elizabeth Rydal, into the spiritual odyssey of Stephen Monk, decided she was his "mother." She is, in fact, a follower of one of the three human paths to salvation: an artist. The second path, chosen by Stephen's second wife, Jane, is that of settling satisfactorily into the life of an ordinary person. The third way, that of sainthood, perhaps lies ahead for Stephen Monk outside the novel. Stephen's foster-mother, Sarah, has achieved a form of sainthood: it is extraordinary with what reality Isherwood manages to endow her, considering that her life is compounded of the sacrifice of earthly passion, the rescue of Nazi victims and smelly dogs, and the preservation of everything, including, in her refrigerator, the half-eaten mice her cat has wisely abandoned.

Elizabeth Rydal, far from being a portrait of Katherine Mansfield—although Kathy, together with Emmy (Brontë) and Wilfred (Owen) were the only writers admired by Isherwood and Chalmers in their early days at Cambridge—is probably the closest Isherwood has come to a self-portrait. Not, of course, a portrait of himself in any obvious way, but a portrait of the humanly suffering individual with the *dharma* of an artist. At any rate, Isherwood has failed, for once, to mock his central character, having perhaps discovered, as Fitzgerald did in *The Great Gatsby*, how to divide his protagonist into the one who suffers and the one who observes.

A Single Man (1964), that masterpiece of a comic novel, is the story of one day in the life of an expatriate English professor in Los Angeles. It contains the best American college classroom scene ever portrayed, and a series of stunning portraits, not least of all George, the central character who, like Leopold Bloom, is allowed no single moment of privacy, but who, unlike Bloom, is not surrounded by a wealth of literary symbols or endowed with a shred more dignity than he can muster up for himself. George is a homosexual, which allows him to have lost his life's companion without being a widower or deserted, and to have a remarkable but largely nonsexual relationship with a woman his own age. What is important about George, and hilariously funny, is that, endowed with that rare gift, life, he goes through his day like an automaton, albeit a lustful one, who might die that night or any night leaving behind him in his bed a body, garbage, and the lost chance of spiritual experience.

Not that *A Single Man* ever mentions spiritual experience; that is its greatness. Here is only the portrait of an inhabited body and the attempts it makes at living. Here is George, the inhabited body, driving to the State College in Los Angeles:

There's always a slightly unpleasant moment when you drive up the ramp which leads onto the freeway and become what's called "merging traffic." George has that nerve-crawling sensation which can't be removed by simply checking the rearview mirror: that, inexplicably, invisibly, he's about to be hit in the back. And then, next moment, he has merged and is away, out in the clear, climbing the long, easy gradient toward the top of the pass and the Valley beyond.

[42]

And now, as he drives, it is as if some kind of autohypnosis exerts itself. We see the face relax, the shoulders unhunch themselves, the body ease itself back into the seat. The reflexes are taking over. . . .

And now something new starts happening to George. The face is becoming tense again, the muscles bulge slightly at the jaw, the mouth tightens and twitches, the lips are pressed together in a firm line, there is a nervous contraction between the eyebrows. And yet, while all this is going on, the rest of the body remains in a posture of perfect relaxation. More and more it appears to separate itself, to become a separate entity: an impassive anonymous chauffeur-figure with little will or individuality of its own, the very embodiment of muscular co-ordination, lack of anxiety, tactful silence, driving its master to work.

And George, like a master who has entrusted the driving of his car to a servant, is now free to direct his attention elsewhere.

Then, when George's attention has been elsewhere for half an hour at least, he finds himself off the freeway:

God! Here we are, downtown already! George comes up dazed to the surface, realizing with a shock that the chauffeur-figure has broken a record: never before has it managed to get them this far entirely on its own. And this raises a disturbing question: Is the chauffeur steadily becoming more and more of an individual? Is it getting ready to take over much larger areas of George's life?

Point of view is the key to the novel's perfection. We watch George as though we were some mocking god, tolerant but supercilious. We move from our godlike vantage point, that perhaps of guardian angel, to inside George whenever George becomes acutely enough aware of his own surroundings. Isherwood's touch never slips. From the college where one can destroy a student by ripping his IBM card, to the beach, the hospital (where George pays a visit), the bars, we have George in exactly the right perspective. Offering absolute delight, *A Single Man* is as funny as Amis's work without burlesquing quite so much. And unlike Amis's novels, *A Single Man* suggests something beyond itself, indicating, in the mirror image of what it presents, what might be possible. This, we might say, is a life without spirit, a life awaiting (through how many life-times like this one?) spiritual experience. But it is not necessary, nor even advisable, to read the book for its suggestions, or to penetrate, past George's hilariously recounted day, to any unstated profundities.

Isherwood's most recent novel, *A Meeting by the River* (1967), is a failure, an attempt to use insufficiently digested material gathered on a visit to a monastery in India. Unable to find the proper narrative technique, as in *A Single Man*, Isherwood falls back on letters which are unsuccessful on even the most superficial level: in an age of telephone calls and jet flights, it is simply improbable that the two brothers in the book would write, for the few days they are together, as compulsively as Clarissa Harlowe. The brother who is about to take his final vows as a monk falls back, sinfully, upon a diary to enable us to learn what we must know. The other brother, a worldly publisher stopping over on his way to Japan for a meeting that could certainly have been more conveniently held in another place at another time, is married and in love with a boy. We see the effect these two have on one another, chiefly the effect the monk has on his worldly brother. Again, the trouble is with sainthood: Isherwood can beautifully repre-sent the charming, lying, ultimately life-enhancing, married, boy-loving publisher. But the connections and repercussions between the two men are insufficiently dramatized. Isherwood might have made a documentary, a sort of travel book, of this material; a novel is impossible, not least because the setting is so exotic as to become invisible. There is a mother (who wor-ries about sanitation and is carefully lied to by her sons), a wife, and two little girls, but all the female characters are offstage, and the reader cannot avoid the conviction that the life of the novel should have taken place in their presence.

[44]

One awaits with eagerness his next book. It is difficult to realize that Isherwood is already in his middle sixties; certainly he gives the sense of having more to produce. He seems to remain so consistently open to experience, all experiences, from drugs to the arduous discipline of religious devotion. One wonders, it is true, what he can possibly be like, and reads with fascination this description of him by Robert Craft, composed in 1949:

> Virginia Woolf's likening Isherwood to a jockey is perfect. Not the clothes, of course . . . but the stature, bantam weight, somewhat too short legs and disproportionately, even simianly long arms. . . . One easily sees Isherwood, or sees how Mrs. Woolf saw him, whether at the pari-mutuel window or the furlong post, as an ornament of the track and the turf.
>
> His manner is casual, vagabondish, lovelorn. One does not readily imagine him in a fit of anger, or behaving precipitately, or enduring extended states of great commotion. At moments he might be thinking of things beyond and remote, from which the conversation brusquely summons him back to earth. But he is a listener and observer—he has the observer's habit of staring—rather than a prepounder and expatiator, and his trance-like eyes will see more deeply through, and record more essential matter about us than this verbosity of mine is doing about him. At the same time, his sense of humor is very ready. He maintains a chronic or semi-permanent smile (a network of small creases about the mouth), supplementing it with giggles and an occasional full-throttle laugh, during which the tongue lolls. (This happens as he tells a story of why he is no longer invited to Chaplin's: "Someone had said I had peed on the sofa there one night while plastered.") But he is not at ease in spite of drollery. Underneath . . . are fears, the uppermost of which might well be of a musical conversation or high general conversation about The Arts.

Now, Craft writes in 1968, "of the old circle of California friends, only Christopher Isherwood survives," and Craft and Igor Stravinsky dedicate *Retrospectives and Conclusions* to him.

He is indeed a survivor. His has been a life of extraordinary adventure, accomplishment, and love: he seems to have meant much to many people. It is, in a sense, ironic that he does not have a central place in the literature of our time, but exists peripherally, still spoken of as one of the Auden, Spender, MacNeice group, or remembered only as the creator of Sally Bowles. But we must remind ourselves that, after all, his life and art seem to have worked continuously toward the extinction of personality, the chief mark of the religion he adopted in 1940 and has practiced for thirty years. In all the articles he has written about Vedanta he has mentioned the symbolic nature of work, the necessity of ignoring its reception, which is not one's business. If his religion of Vedanta simply has not worked when incorporated wholesale into his novels (as in *A Meeting by the River*) it appears to have worked well enough in his life and therefore indirectly in his art. Certainly it is essential for anyone who would understand him to realize that his religious conversion has made him closer to, not more distant from, the problems of his time.

For he has been, as Angus Wilson has said, close to the moral center of his generation. "Again and again," Wilson writes, "Berlin, America, California and the Ghita—he has stepped over the edge that we have run away from, yet his literary stature has grown and so, too, has the depth of vision he offers us. . . . For those of us who cling to our more rational, provincial and conventional ways," the maddening thing is not only, as Wilson suggests, that our mixed reaction of jealousy, admiration, disapproval, and embarrassment is precisely that "with which we should receive a saint if ever we should meet one." Maddening, too, is the realization that in failing to appreciate Isherwood we have failed to understand ourselves.

SELECTED BIBLIOGRAPHY

NOTE: Christopher Isherwood: A Bibliography, 1923–1967 *has been published by the California State College at Los Angeles Foundation.*

Principal Works of Christopher Isherwood

All the Conspirators. London, Jonathan Cape, 1928. Paperback edition, London, Sphere Books, 1967.

The Memorial. London, Hogarth Press, 1932. New Edition, Hogarth Press, 1960.

Mr. Norris Changes Trains. London, Hogarth Press, 1935. (Published in the United States as The Last of Mr. Norris, 1935.)

Sally Bowles. London, Hogarth Press, 1937.

Lions and Shadows. London, Hogarth Press, 1938. London, New English Library, 1963.

Journey to a War. London, Faber and Faber, 1939.

Goodbye to Berlin. London, Hogarth Press, 1939.

Prater Violet. New York, Random House, 1945.

Berlin Stories (The Last of Mr. Norris; Sally Bowles; Goodbye to Berlin). New York, New Directions, 1945. New Directions Paperback, 1963.

The Condor and the Cows. New York, Random House, 1949.

The World in the Evening. New York, Random House, 1954.

Down There on a Visit. New York. Simon and Schuster, 1962.

An Approach to Vedanta. Hollywood, Vedanta Press, 1963.

A Single Man. New York, Simon and Schuster, 1964.

Ramakrishna and His Disciples. New York, Simon and Schuster, 1965.

Exhumations. New York, Simon and Schuster, 1966.

A Meeting by the River. New York, Simon and Schuster, 1967.

Critical Works and Commentary

Hampshire, Stuart. "Isherwood's Hell," *Encounter*, November, 1962, pp. 86–88.

Kermode, Frank. "The Interpretation of the Times," in Puzzles and Epiphanies, pp. 121–30. London, Routledge and Kegan Paul, 1962.

Lehmann, John. In My Own Time. Boston, Little, Brown, 1969.

Poss, Stanley. "A Conversation on Tape," *London Magazine*, June, 1961, pp. 41–58.

Spender, Stephen. World Within World. New York, Harcourt, Brace & World, 1951.

Whitehead, John. "Christophananda Isherwood at Sixty," *London Magazine*, July, 1965, pp. 90–100.

Wickes, George. "An Interview with Christopher Isherwood," *Shenandoah*, Spring, 1965, pp. 22–52.

Wilson, Angus. "The New and the Old Isherwood," *Encounter*, August, 1954, pp. 63–68.

———— Review of Exhumations, *Observer*, March 20, 1966, p. 26.

ATE DUE